Healthy relationships

How to improve communication
and strengthen personal and romantic relationships.

Phillip A. Johansen

Anuket Editorial

Have you ever felt like your words aren't enough to express your feelings? Have you ever wondered why some relationships wear out over time?

Like many of us, I've experienced the ups and downs of interpersonal relationships. Through my experiences and studies, I've discovered that communication is the key to building lasting connections. In this book, I invite you to explore the transformative power of words and learn how to improve your communication skills to strengthen your personal and loving relationships.

As the Roman philosopher Seneca said, "Communication is the source of all evil and all good."

Get ready to embark on a journey toward deeper, more fulfilling relationships.

Contents:
1. Types of relationships: their importance
2. Fundamentals of a healthy relationship
3. The magic of effective communication
4. Managing conflicts in a healthy way
5. Building emotional intimacy
6. Growing Together: Promoting individual and couple development
7. Breaking toxic patterns and healing the relationship

Chapter 1
Types of Relationships:
Their Importance

Interpersonal relationships enrich our lives and give us a sense of belonging. However, we often find ourselves facing challenges in our interactions with others. As Zygmunt Bauman noted, 'Liquid modernity has made relationships fragile and ephemeral.' This book will help you build stronger, more meaningful relationships, providing you with the tools necessary to navigate the challenges of modern life."

Healthy, caring personal relationships are essential to emotional well-being and overall life satisfaction. These relationships, defined by characteristics such as mutual respect, trust, effective communication, empathy, and vulnerability, foster a supportive environment that enhances individual happiness and promotes longevity.

Research indicates that healthy interpersonal connections are linked to better mental and physical health outcomes, including lower levels of stress and a lower risk of chronic disease, highlighting their importance in maintaining a balanced life.

Various types of relationships—romantic, friendships, parent-child dynamics, sibling bonds, professional connections, and mentoring relationships—serve unique purposes and contribute to an individual's emotional landscape.

In romantic relationships, for example, open communication about intimacy and a shared commitment to mutual growth can significantly enhance emotional fulfillment and self-esteem.

Similarly, healthy friendships provide essential emotional support and companionship, while positive family relationships lay the foundation for an individual's future interpersonal connections.

Despite their benefits, healthy relationships can face challenges such as communication breakdowns, external stressors, and emotional barriers, which can lead to conflict and tension.

Recognizing signs of relationship deterioration, such as feelings of contempt or lack of open dialogue, is critical for couples who wish to maintain their bond. Strategies to foster healthy relationships include active listening, setting boundaries, and seeking professional help when necessary, all of which can help mitigate conflict and reinforce connection.

The interconnection between mental health and relationship quality underscores the importance of fostering these bonds. People who have supportive relationships tend to show higher levels of happiness and productivity, while a lack of social connections can lead to greater feelings of loneliness and cognitive decline.

Ultimately, cultivating healthy, caring personal relationships not only improves individual well-being but also contributes positively to the overall fabric of society.

Types of Healthy Relationships

Healthy relationships can take many forms, each serving a specific function in people's lives. Understanding the different types of healthy relationships can help people cultivate and maintain them effectively.

• Romantic Relationships

Romantic relationships play a crucial role in human life. Since time immemorial, the search for emotional, physical, and spiritual connection with another person has been a central part of the human experience. These relationships not only influence the emotional and psychological well-being of individuals but also impact the structure and functioning of society as a whole.

1. The Impact of Romantic Relationships on Men

For men, romantic relationships can provide a vital space for emotional expression, support, and personal growth. Culturally, men often face pressures to be emotionally reserved or to come on strong, which can lead to difficulties in processing and communicating their feelings. However, in a healthy romantic relationship, men can find a safe space to explore and express those emotions, contributing to a more balanced psychological well-being.

Key Benefits:

Stress reduction: A healthy romantic relationship can act as an emotional buffer. Having someone to rely on and share daily challenges with reduces stress and promotes greater emotional well-being.

<u>Emotional support</u>: Romantic relationships offer men an environment in which they can feel understood and supported, which can be especially important during times of personal or professional difficulty.

<u>Emotional development</u>: Emotional intimacy in a relationship allows men to develop their emotional intelligence, something that is often overlooked due to societal norms. Learning to empathize, listen, and be vulnerable strengthens interpersonal skills, which can also positively influence other areas of life, such as work and friendships.

However, when relationships are unhealthy, men may face mental health issues, and anxiety, or feel trapped in emotional dependency dynamics or unresolved conflicts. Gender expectations, which often require them to be the "protector" or "provider," can create internal tensions, highlighting the need for romantic relationships to be based on mutual support rather than rigid traditional roles.

2. The impact of romantic relationships on women
For women, romantic relationships are also deeply meaningful, both emotionally and practically. Throughout history, romantic relationships and marriages have played a crucial role in women's lives, from emotional support to the traditional role of raising a family. Today, women seek relationships that are more egalitarian and offer space for individual and joint growth.

Key benefits:

<u>Emotional support and connection:</u> Women tend to value emotional intimacy in relationships, and this closeness provides them with an important source of support and security. In a healthy relationship, women can feel heard, respected, and valued, which contributes to a greater sense of self-esteem and well-being.

<u>Personal and professional growth:</u> In many relationships, mutual support is key to women feeling empowered to pursue their professional and personal aspirations. A partner who encourages growth and independence can be a driver for individual success.

<u>Mental and physical health:</u> Studies have shown that women in healthy romantic relationships tend to have fewer problems with anxiety and depression, which is due in part to the consistent emotional support and sense of security that these relationships provide.

However, when relationships are inequitable or fraught with conflict, women may face emotional stress and feelings of low self-esteem. Cultural expectations that demand that women take on "caretaker" roles within the relationship or household can lead to excessive emotional burdens if responsibilities are not distributed fairly.

3. The impact of romantic relationships on society
Beyond the effects on individual well-being, romantic relationships have a significant impact on society. These relationships are the foundations upon which

families, communities, and ultimately the social structure are formed. Romantic relationships influence the values, norms, and behaviors that are passed down through generations.

Key social aspects:

<u>Family formation</u>: Romantic relationships are often the foundation of family formation, a fundamental nucleus in any society. The family dynamics that arise from these relationships impact child rearing, economic structures, and community connections.

<u>Social stability</u>: Healthy romantic relationships contribute to social stability by fostering commitment, mutual respect, and cooperation. Couples who manage to maintain a strong relationship also tend to become more involved in the community, promoting social cohesion.

<u>Transmission of values</u>: Through romantic relationships and family ties, important values are transmitted, such as empathy, cooperation, respect, and responsibility. These values spread throughout society and reinforce peaceful coexistence and respect for others.

In recent years, romantic relationships have begun to change in response to emerging social and economic dynamics. Gender expectations in relationships have evolved, allowing for greater equity and opportunities for personal development for both partners. These new dynamics contribute to a more egalitarian society, where men and women can share responsibilities at home and work, which has a positive impact on family and social well-being.

The impact of romantic relationships on well-being is not only emotional but also physical. Numerous studies have shown that people in committed and stable relationships tend to live longer and have fewer physical and mental health problems.

What Toxic Relationships Negatively Affect Society

While healthy romantic relationships have a positive impact, toxic or destructive relationships can have profound negative effects. Unresolved conflict, domestic violence, emotional manipulation, and abuse are problems that not only affect individuals but also have repercussions at a societal level.

Consequences of toxic relationships:

Impact on mental health: Toxic relationships can lead to high levels of stress, depression, anxiety, and emotional trauma that affect overall well-being.

Family disintegration: Destructive conflicts within relationships can lead to separation or divorce, which can have a lasting impact on children and family stability.

Domestic violence: Violence in relationships severely affects society, placing a burden on health, judicial, and social welfare systems. The consequences of domestic violence extend beyond couples, affecting children and communities.

Romantic relationships are fundamental pillars for the emotional and physical well-being of individuals, as well as for the stability and cohesion of society. The emotional bonds formed in these relationships have the power to transform lives, providing support, stability, and a sense of belonging. However, these relationships must be based on mutual respect, fairness, and emotional support so that they can thrive and have a positive impact on people's lives and society at large.

A healthy romantic relationship not only improves the lives of the individuals involved, but also contributes to a more just, balanced, and supportive society, where common well-being is built on the foundations of love, respect, and mutual commitment.

Romantic relationships involve a deep emotional bond and often include elements such as intimacy and trust. Characteristics of a healthy romantic relationship include open communication about intimacy and a mutual desire to support and grow together.

The positive effects of healthy romantic relationships extend beyond emotional satisfaction and contribute to individual self-esteem and social integration.

Communication, empathy, respect, and commitment are essential to maintaining the health of such relationships.

- **Friendship**

Friendship relationships are one of the fundamental pillars of emotional and psychological well-being in people's lives. Throughout history, friendship has been recognized as one of the deepest forms of human connection, providing support, companionship, and a sense of belonging. Unlike family or romantic relationships, friendship is a bond that is freely chosen, making it a reflection of shared values and genuine affection.

1. The Emotional Value of Friendship

Friendship brings emotional value that transcends words. Friends are the people with whom we share our joys, sorrows, successes, and failures, and their presence in our lives has a direct effect on our happiness and mental well-being. Through friendships, we experience a unique form of emotional connection, as these relationships are often based on reciprocity, respect, and trust.

Emotional Benefits of Friendship:

<u>Support in difficult times:</u> Friends are often our first source of support when we face challenges. Sharing our worries and anxieties with a trusted friend can relieve stress and provide comfort.

<u>Mood enhancement:</u> Interactions with friends have a positive impact on mood. Laughing, talking, or simply spending time together generates a feeling of joy and connection that strengthens emotional well-being.

13

Reducing loneliness: Loneliness is one of the biggest risk factors for mental health. Friendship helps combat it by providing a space where people feel valued, supported, and understood.

2. Friendship and mental health

Friendship relationships are not only important for emotional well-being, but they also play an essential role in mental health. Maintaining close and meaningful friendships reduces the risk of depression, anxiety, and other mental disorders. Friendship also contributes to emotional resilience, as friends provide a support network that can help people face difficult times with greater strength.

How friendship affects mental health:

Active listening and empathy: Friends who know how to listen without judging and offer empathy help people process their emotions and find solutions to their problems. This type of emotional support is crucial to maintaining mental health.

Preventing social isolation: Social isolation is a major risk factor for the development of mental health problems. Friendships allow for constant interaction that counteracts isolation and fosters a sense of community.

Stress reduction: Social activities with friends, such as going for a walk, chatting, or doing recreational activities, are effective ways to reduce stress and promote relaxation.

3. Friendship in personal development

Beyond emotional support and mental health, friendships also play a crucial role in personal development. Friends not only help us feel understood, but they also challenge us to grow, explore new interests, and reflect on our life experiences. Through friendship, people can broaden their perspectives and learn from each other's experiences and knowledge.

The impact of friendship on personal growth:

<u>Development of social skills</u>: Friendships allow people to practice social skills such as communication, empathy, conflict resolution, and collaboration. These skills not only strengthen friendships but are also useful in other areas of life, such as work and family relationships.

<u>Reinforcement of self-esteem</u>: Having friends who value and appreciate who we are increases our self-esteem. Mutual support and recognition in a friendship help each person feel valued and accepted as they are.

<u>Continuous learning</u>: Friendships allow for the exchange of ideas, perspectives, and knowledge. Friends can motivate each other to learn new things, try new experiences, and pursue goals they might not have otherwise considered.

4. Friendship at different stages of life

The value of friendship varies depending on the stage of life, but its importance persists at all stages. From infancy to old age, friendships serve different functions that adapt to the needs and circumstances of each stage.

In childhood, friendships are fundamental to emotional and social development. Children learn to share, cooperate, and resolve conflicts through their interactions with friends.

In adolescence, friendships take on a new dimension as young people seek independence and build their identity through relationships with their peers. These friendships are essential for the development of healthy self-esteem and a sense of belonging.

In adulthood, friendships continue to provide emotional support, but they also help balance the responsibilities of daily life. At this stage, friendships are often based on shared interests, life goals, and similar experiences.

Adult friendships can be a source of comfort in times of crisis, such as during work problems, family changes, or personal losses.

In old age, friendships play a crucial role in combating loneliness and social isolation. Friendships at this stage provide companionship, emotional support, and a sense of belonging, which is critical to maintaining a sense of purpose and well-being in life.

5. The social impact of friendship

Beyond their benefits, friendships also have a significant impact on society. Friendship networks form a strong foundation for social cohesion, promoting values such as empathy, collaboration, and solidarity. Strong communities are often made up of individuals who value and cultivate meaningful interpersonal relationships, including friendships.

Social aspects of friendship:

<u>Fostering social cohesion</u>: Friendships help create connections between people of different backgrounds and perspectives, which promotes greater understanding and tolerance. These types of bonds can strengthen social cohesion and reduce division between groups.

<u>Promoting empathy and solidarity:</u> Friendships teach people to be more empathetic and caring. Through friendships, we learn to value the experiences of others and offer our support when needed.

<u>Building support networks</u>: Friendships form support networks in communities, facilitating the sharing of resources, knowledge, and mutual assistance. This is especially important in crises, where people may rely on their friends for help.

Friendships are much more than just social connections; they are a vital driver of emotional well-being, personal growth, and social cohesion. Friends not only accompany us through the most important moments of life, but they also provide unconditional support, challenge us to be better people, and help us navigate the complexities of life.

Healthy friendships are characterized by trust, respect, and mutual enjoyment, making them an essential component of a fulfilling life. Reconnecting with friends can be especially beneficial, as these relationships can enhance overall well-being.

• Parent-child relationships

The relationship between parents and children is one of the most fundamental and significant bonds in a person's life. From birth, this connection is essential for children's emotional, social, and cognitive development, while for parents it represents a source of personal satisfaction and growth. The quality of this relationship profoundly influences the formation of children's identity, emotional well-being, and social skills, shaping their ability to face life in a healthy and balanced way.

1. Foundation of emotional development
The relationship with parents is the first emotional bond a child experiences. Through consistent interaction with their parents, children learn to identify and regulate their emotions. Parents who offer a caring, safe, and supportive environment foster confidence and healthy emotional development in their children. This not only reinforces self-esteem but also helps children cope with their emotional challenges throughout life.

2. Development of social and cognitive skills
Parents act as their children's first teachers, providing not only basic knowledge but also models of social behavior. The parent-child relationship teaches children skills such as empathy, cooperation, and effective communication. In addition, parental involvement in their children's education and learning

stimulates their cognitive development, preparing them for academic and professional success in the future.

3. Construction of identity and values
Throughout their growth, children observe and absorb the values, beliefs, and behaviors of their parents. A strong, positive relationship provides a firm foundation on which children can build their identity. Parents who instill principles such as respect, responsibility, and compassion help to form confident, well-adjusted individuals who contribute positively to society.

4. Support in adult life
Although the relationship between parents and children evolves, it remains a crucial source of support in adult life. The guidance, advice, and affection that parents continue to offer their adult children help maintain strong family bonds and provide a sense of stability and continuity in an ever-changing world.

The relationship between parents and children is fundamental to the emotional well-being and comprehensive development of children. A bond based on love, understanding, and communication is crucial to forming individuals who are secure, empathetic, and prepared to face life's challenges. For parents, this bond represents an unparalleled opportunity to positively influence the future of their children, leaving a legacy in their development as people.

• Relationships between siblings

The relationship between siblings is one of the most lasting and significant connections in a person's life. From childhood to adulthood, siblings share unique experiences, memories, and moments that especially unite them. This bond, often characterized by closeness, trust, and mutual support, has a profound impact on the emotional, social, and personal development of individuals.

1. Emotional and social development

Siblings are the first playmates and often the first friends we have. Through our relationship with them, we learn important lessons about living together, sharing, and conflict resolution. Sibling interactions help children develop key social skills such as empathy, negotiation, and cooperation, preparing them for future relationships in life.

2. Mutual Support and Resilience

Throughout life, siblings can be a constant source of emotional support. During times of difficulty or crisis, having a sibling can provide comfort and security. This relationship creates a safe space where vulnerability can be expressed without fear of judgment, promoting resilience in the face of challenges.

3. Identity Formation

Siblings also play an important role in building personal identity. By sharing family, cultural, and emotional experiences, siblings influence how we see ourselves and how we relate to the world. Through their differences and similarities, siblings help us define our personalities and better understand who we are.

4. Lifelong Relationship

While other relationships may change or fade, the relationship between siblings often endures throughout life. As people grow and face different life stages, siblings provide a bond that evolves, offering companionship, support, and understanding at every phase of life.

The relationship between siblings is a unique bond that deeply influences a person's emotional and social development. Forged in childhood and able to strengthen over time, this bond offers a space for mutual support, understanding, and personal growth. Siblings are not only life partners, but also a source of comfort, learning, and unconditional love.

• Professional relationships

Relationships with coworkers and superiors are essential for personal and professional development. Healthy professional relationships are based on respect, collaboration, and open communication. They can improve job satisfaction and foster a positive work environment, which is beneficial for mental health and career advancement.

• Mentoring relationships

Mentoring involves a more experienced person guiding a less experienced person. Healthy mentoring relationships are characterized by trust, mutual respect, and open communication, leading to personal and professional growth for both parties.

Chapter 2
Fundamentals
of a Healthy Relationship

Healthy relationships are characterized by mutual respect, communication, and understanding of individual needs. These relationships not only enhance personal well-being but also positively contribute to overall health and longevity. According to research, people in healthy relationships tend to engage in healthier and more balanced behaviors, which leads to experiencing better health outcomes, resulting in a longer and happier life.

Characteristics of Healthy Relationships

A healthy relationship is characterized by several key features:

Open communication: Effective communication is essential and encompasses not only the exchange of words but also active listening and nonverbal cues. It allows the interlocutors to express their thoughts and feelings clearly, which fosters understanding and reduces misunderstandings.

Respect for boundaries: Establishing and maintaining healthy boundaries is critical. Each person should feel comfortable expressing their needs and boundaries, which helps cultivate a sense of security and individuality within the relationship.

<u>Empathy and understanding:</u> A strong relationship thrives on empathy, where partners strive to see the world from each other's perspectives. This approach mitigates conflict and fosters a deeper emotional connection.

Empathy plays a critical role in maintaining healthy relationships. It involves the ability to understand and share another person's feelings, allowing for deeper emotional bonds and building trust.

For example, when one partner experiences stress, responding with empathy rather than disdain can significantly strengthen the bond between them. Research indicates that couples who prioritize empathy and effective communication report higher levels of satisfaction in their relationships.

<u>Supporting individual growth:</u> Healthy relationships encourage both partners to pursue their interests and goals. Maintaining individuality while growing together strengthens the bond and contributes to mutual satisfaction.

<u>Team problem-solving:</u> Collaboratively facing challenges and embracing each other's differences can help build resilience in the relationship. Working together not only solves problems but also strengthens the foundation of the partnership.

Basic Principles of Relationships

The dynamics of healthy relationships also depend on several basic principles, including uniqueness and mutual commitment. Uniqueness refers to how relationship outcomes are determined not only by the individual qualities of the partners but also by the unique patterns that emerge from their interactions. This means that relationships can develop a life of their own, independent of the individuals involved, influencing satisfaction and overall well-being.

Furthermore, mutual commitment has been shown to lead to better well-being outcomes, as demonstrated in partnerships where both parties are actively involved in maintaining and nurturing the relationship.

Psychological and Emotional Well-Being

Healthy relationships contribute positively to mental and physical health. Positive social bonds and nurturing relationships are protective factors against mental health problems and can promote overall brain health.

Conversely, chronic emotional stress caused by unhealthy relationships can lead to a variety of health problems, including an increased risk of heart disease.

The interconnection between psychological well-being and relational health highlights the importance of cultivating satisfying interpersonal connections throughout life.

Reflecting on Social Norms

Understanding the social norms that govern interpersonal interactions can also improve relationship dynamics. Social influence can shape behaviors and attitudes within relationships, indicating that knowledge of these norms can lead to healthier interactions.

Incorporating these strategies can significantly improve the quality of personal and romantic relationships, making them more resilient in the face of challenges.

Challenges for Healthy Relationships

Healthy relationships can face various challenges that can affect their overall quality and longevity over time. Understanding these challenges is essential for couples to effectively deal with them.

A strong and healthy relationship is built on three fundamental pillars: trust, mutual respect, and open communication. These principles act as the foundations of a lasting relationship, whether romantic, familial, or friendly. However, often, our ideas about love and expectations for a relationship are colored by common myths that do not fit reality.

Below, we'll explore these essential pillars and debunk some of the most prevalent myths about love, to offer a more realistic perspective for a lasting relationship.

1. Trust: The Foundation of Emotional Intimacy

Trust is perhaps the most important pillar of any relationship. Without it, it's impossible to develop a deep and meaningful connection. Trust is built over time, through consistent actions and honesty. It involves believing, based on evidence, that the other person acts with good intentions and that they keep their commitments and promises. However, it's important to note that trust is neither automatic nor permanent. It's a constant build that requires mutual effort. Trust is not given, it's earned.

Myth: "If you truly love someone, you'll always trust them blindly."

Reality: Trust isn't based on blind faith but on experience and consistency. We're all human and can make mistakes, so trust also involves being able to forgive and rebuild when there are failures, as long as there's a genuine commitment to improve.

2. Mutual Respect: The Value of Differences

Respect is essential for a relationship to be equitable and healthy. Respecting your partner doesn't mean agreeing on everything, but valuing their thoughts, feelings, and perspectives, even when they differ from yours. Respect creates an environment where both partners can freely express themselves without fear of judgment or rejection.

Myth: "True love involves agreeing on everything."

Reality: Differences of opinion are natural and healthy. Mutual respect allows couples to have constructive discussions without feeling attacked. Instead of always seeking unanimity, respect teaches people to value diversity of thoughts as an opportunity to grow together.

3. Open Communication: The Art of Expressing and Listening

Communication is the bridge that connects two people in any relationship. It's not just about talking, but about expressing needs, feelings, and concerns clearly and honestly, without fear of being judged. But communication isn't just about talking, it also involves actively listening, being willing to understand, and asking questions to clear up any misunderstandings.

Myth: "If he loves me, he'll know what I need without me saying it."

Reality: This is one of the most destructive myths in relationships. People are not mind readers, and expecting your partner to guess what you feel or need only creates frustration. Open and honest communication allows expectations and desires to be clearly expressed, reducing the scope for misunderstandings and resentments.

It is common, especially among women, to believe that their partner should understand them with a simple glance, just as their father did in childhood. That is impossible, neither is she a child, nor is he an adult deciphering a child.

4. Realistic expectations for a lasting relationship

One of the main obstacles in modern relationships is unrealistic expectations, often influenced by movies, television, and social media. It is easy to fall into the trap of idealizing perfection in a couple or a relationship, believing that true love never has problems or disagreements.

Myth: "Happy relationships don't have conflict."
Reality: All relationships, no matter how healthy, face challenges and conflicts. The secret is not to avoid problems but to learn to handle them constructively. The ability to resolve disagreements, listen to each other's points of view, and reach compromises strengthens the relationship in the long run. Instead of seeing conflicts as a sign of failure, we should see them as opportunities to grow together.

5. Demystifying Romantic Love: Beyond Initial Passion

Romantic love is often depicted as a passionate, constant thrill. However, that initial phase of falling in love, filled with intense emotions and butterflies in the stomach, is not sustainable in the long run. Real love is a daily choice that involves commitment, effort, and mutual sacrifices. The same goes for friendship but without the romantic ingredient.

Myth: "True love is always passionate and exciting."
Reality: Love matures and evolves. What begins as an initial spark of passion transforms into a deeper connection based on friendship, companionship, and respect. Couples who understand this are better able to cultivate a long-term relationship, where emotional intimacy and commitment become more important than mere emotion.

Other great myths about love

Myths about romantic love are beliefs rooted in our culture that often lead us to have unrealistic expectations about relationships. These excessive expectations can lead to frustration, disillusionment, and in some cases, even the end of a relationship.

Some of the most common myths are:

Love can do anything: It is believed that love can solve any problem and overcoming any obstacle, which is not always the case.

Love at first sight: The idea that true love arises instantly and perfectly, without the need to know the other person in depth.

The better half: The belief that there is only one person destined for each of us, who complements us perfectly and makes us feel complete.

The couple must satisfy all our needs: Expecting our partner to be our best friend, lover, confidant, and companion always.

The couple must not change: Expecting our partner to remain the same over time, without allowing personal growth and the evolution of the relationship.

Jealousy is proof of love: Believing that jealousy is a demonstration of affection and possession towards the partner.

The couple must dedicate all their time to us: Expecting our partner to give up their interests and friendships to always be available for us.

The relationship must be perfect: Believing that a relationship must be free of conflicts and disagreements.

Love must last forever: Assuming that romantic love will always be intense and passionate throughout life.

Why are these myths harmful?

They generate frustration: Not finding in reality what is expected of an idealized relationship, produces great frustration.

They hinder communication: By assuming that the partner must read the mind, open and honest communication is prevented.

They create unrealistic expectations: By having expectations that are too high, any imperfection in the relationship can be seen as a failure.

They encourage dependency: By believing that the partner must satisfy all our needs, personal autonomy is lost.

How can we overcome these myths?

Be realistic: Understand that relationships are complex and require effort and commitment from both partners.

<u>Communicate openly</u>: Express our needs, feelings, and expectations clearly and honestly.

<u>Cultivate individuality</u>: Keep our interests and friendships outside the relationship.

<u>Accept changes</u>: Understand that people and relationships change over time.

<u>Work on the relationship</u>: Invest time and energy in strengthening the relationship.

Love as a joint effort

A strong relationship does not happen by accident; it is the result of constant effort from both parties. Myths about love can create unrealistic expectations and make it difficult to develop healthy, long-lasting relationships. By being aware of these myths and working on building relationships based on communication, respect, and reality, we can enjoy more satisfying and long-lasting relationships. By banishing harmful myths about love and adopting realistic expectations, we can actively work to build relationships that not only last over time but also enrich us as people.

Relationships are not based on perfection but on the genuine connection between two people who choose to grow together.

Chapter 3
The Magic
of Effective Communication

Communication is at the heart of any relationship. However, it is not enough to just talk; the quality of what is said and how it is said is crucial. Assertive communication stands as a key element to maintaining healthy personal and loving relationships, where both parties feel understood, respected, and valued.

Assertive communication not only strengthens relationships but also makes them more resilient in the face of challenges. By learning to express needs clearly, avoid misunderstandings, and actively listen, a constructive dialogue is fostered that allows both parties to grow together. Implementing these keys consciously not only improves the quality of the relationship but also the emotional well-being of those who make it up.

Next, we will explore the keys to effective communication, how to express needs clearly, avoid misunderstandings, and actively listen to foster a constructive dialogue.

1. The importance of assertiveness in relationships
Assertiveness is the ability to express our thoughts, feelings, and needs clearly and respectfully, without imposing or giving in to the demands of the other. In personal and romantic relationships, assertiveness is vital because it allows us to communicate our

expectations and limits without aggression or passivity, generating a more authentic and honest connection.

What does it mean to be assertive? Being assertive involves finding the balance between expressing what we feel without hurting others or being subjected to their opinions. That is, defending our opinions and rights, but without attacking or devaluing the other person.

2. How to express needs clearly

One of the pillars of assertive communication is clarity in the expression of our needs. In many relationships, misunderstandings, and frustrations arise when one of the parties does not adequately communicate what they expect or need. It is crucial to stop assuming that our partner or friend "should know" what we need (especially when, sometimes, we are not even clear about our needs), and instead, learn to express those desires directly and honestly.

Techniques for clear expression:

Use "I" instead of "you": Instead of saying "You never listen to me," try "I feel ignored when you don't pay attention to what I say." This prevents the other person from feeling attacked and promotes a more open dialogue.

Be specific: Avoid generalizations like "always" or "never." If something bothers you, be specific. "I was upset that you didn't tell me you were going to be late yesterday" is clearer and more manageable than "You never tell me about anything."

<u>Speak at the right time:</u> Choose opportune moments to address important topics. It's not a good idea to discuss sensitive issues when one of the parties is angry or tired, as this can lead to defensive reactions.

3. How to avoid misunderstandings in communication

Misunderstandings are inevitable in any relationship, but many of them can be avoided with good communication. Often, these misunderstandings occur when we assume we know what the other person is thinking or feel like we're not being heard.

Tips to avoid misunderstandings:

<u>Ask clarifying questions:</u> Instead of jumping to conclusions, ask the other person what they meant or how they felt. A simple "What did you mean by that?" or "Did something in particular bother you?" can avoid a lot of confusion.

<u>Avoid assumptions:</u> Assumptions can lead to unnecessary conflict. If you're not clear about the intent or meaning behind your partner or friend's actions or words, it's better to ask directly than to jump to conclusions.

<u>Repeat or paraphrase what you heard:</u> This technique, called "mirroring," involves repeating back what the other person said to make sure you understood it correctly. For example, if your partner says to you, "I feel overwhelmed," you might respond, "I understand that you feel overwhelmed, can you tell me more about that?"

4. Active listening: More than hearing, it's about understanding

Active listening is one of the most powerful skills in assertive communication. It's not just about hearing what the other person is saying, but about paying full attention, showing empathy, and responding in a way that makes the other party feel understood. Taking the time to understand your partner's thoughts can lead to a more harmonious connection.

How to practice active listening:

<u>Show genuine interest</u>: Maintain eye contact, nod, and use verbal expressions like "I understand" or "continue" to show that you're engaged in the conversation.

<u>Avoid interrupting</u>: Even if you feel like you have an immediate answer, wait for the other person to finish speaking before giving your opinion. Interruptions can make the other party feel like their point of view isn't important.

<u>Watch nonverbal language:</u> Often, words don't say everything. Pay attention to the other person's facial expressions, tone of voice, and body language to pick up on their emotions and implicit messages.

<u>Practice empathy</u>: Putting yourself in someone else's shoes is essential for effective communication. Try to understand how your conversation partner feels and demonstrate that understanding with comments like, "I can imagine how frustrating this must be for you."

<u>Side-by-side conversations:</u> Engaging in side-by-side conversations (such as walking or biking together) can make difficult discussions more manageable. These settings can help people communicate more clearly and effectively about difficult topics.

5. Encourage constructive dialogue

Assertive communication doesn't just involve speaking up and listening, but also building a dialogue that is productive for both parties. This means that both people in the relationship should feel comfortable sharing their views without fear of being judged or belittled.

Key elements of constructive dialogue:

<u>Create a safe environment:</u> Make sure the other person feels comfortable and free to speak up. Avoid destructive criticism or sarcastic comments, as these can inhibit the other person's willingness to open.

<u>Seek joint solutions:</u> If a problem arises, focus on finding solutions rather than assigning blame. The phrase "How can we solve this together?" is much more effective than "This is all your fault."

<u>Accept differences:</u> You won't always reach a total agreement, and that's okay. Mutual respect means accepting that the other person has a right to a different perspective.

<u>Set boundaries:</u> Establishing individual spaces is vital to maintaining respect in the relationship. Guidelines about acceptable behavior (such as prohibiting yelling or physical aggression) can prevent conflicts from

escalating. Respecting boundaries ensures that disagreements don't spiral out of control.

<u>Apology</u>: Acknowledging mistakes can go a long way toward mending rifts in a relationship. A simple apology—acknowledging one's role in a disagreement—can pave the way to healing, even if it's not an admission of wrongdoing but rather an acknowledgment of shared feelings.

<u>Benefit of the doubt:</u> Offering the benefit of the doubt is critical to fostering a loving relationship. By trying to understand the partner's perspective, people can foster empathy and reduce potential conflict.

Remember, healthy, loving personal relationships require consistent effort and effective communication.

Chapter 4
Managing Conflict
in a Healthy Way

In every relationship, differences and conflicts are inevitable. Two people, with different experiences, perspectives, and expectations, will inevitably face moments of tension. However, how a couple handles these conflicts is what truly defines the quality and longevity of the relationship. Instead of seeing disagreements as threats, they can be understood as opportunities to strengthen the bond, learn to negotiate and foster empathy.

Below, key strategies are developed to resolve conflicts without damaging the relationship, promoting a healthier and longer-lasting connection.

Common Causes of Conflict

Conflicts in relationships can have multiple origins. One of the main causes is communication problems, which can lead to misunderstandings and ineffective listening.

Partners often have different communication styles, making it difficult to express thoughts and emotions clearly. For example, while one partner may prefer direct communication, the other may rely more on nonverbal cues, leading to frustration and confusion. Individual differences in values, beliefs, and personalities can also contribute to disagreements.

Partners may come from different backgrounds, leading to different perspectives that can conflict, especially when core values are at stake.

Recognizing and respecting each other's individuality, practicing empathy, and identifying shared values can help mitigate these conflicts.

External stressors

External factors such as work pressure, financial hardship, and health issues can further exacerbate conflicts within a relationship. These stressors can create additional tensions that partners must manage, sometimes causing unresolved past issues to resurface and affect the current dynamic.

Couples need to identify and address these external stressors to maintain a healthy connection—most importantly, to not forget why they decided to be together, which is at the core of the relationship.

Emotional barriers

Emotional intelligence plays a critical role in how couples manage conflicts. For example, assumptions about a partner's intentions can lead to misunderstandings and increased tension.

Maintaining a positive attitude and assuming positive intentions can help reduce the likelihood of conflict. Couples should strive to communicate effectively using "I" statements and making requests rather than complaints, which encourages more constructive dialogue.

Recognizing Relationship Health

Couples must recognize signs that a relationship is deteriorating, such as the need to censor one's thoughts or fear of negative reactions from their partner. If one partner rejects or shows contempt for the other's viewpoints, it can be a sign of disrespect and create an unsafe environment for open communication.

Seeking professional help or talking to a trusted friend can be beneficial in addressing these concerns and assessing whether the relationship can be saved, or improved, or if it is time to move on separately.

By actively recognizing and addressing these challenges, couples can work to foster a healthier, more satisfying relationship.

Myths and Truths About Relationships

1. Understand that conflict is natural

One of the biggest myths surrounding relationships is that a happy couple doesn't have conflict. Conflict is a natural part of any close relationship, as each person brings with them their own set of beliefs, values, and ways of doing things. The important thing is not to avoid disagreements, but to learn to handle them constructively.

Myth: "If we fight, it means something is wrong in our relationship."

Reality: How the couple resolves conflicts is more important than the conflict itself. The healthiest couples are not those who never argue, but those who approach their differences with respect and a willingness to find a solution.

2. The Key to Effective Conflict Resolution: Communication and Respect

Respect and effective communication are the pillars of resolving any conflict without damaging the relationship. Both partners must feel heard and respected, even when their points of view differ. This requires developing skills such as active listening, assertiveness, and empathy.

Tips for respectful communication amid conflict:

<u>Avoid insults and personal criticism:</u> It's easy to get carried away by emotions and fall into the trap of insulting or criticizing the other person. Phrases like "You're selfish" or "You always do the same thing" attack the personality rather than the problem. Instead, focus on the specific behavior that bothers you: "I felt hurt when you didn't consult me before making that decision."

<u>Be aware of tone and body language:</u> The way something is said sometimes carries more weight than what is said. Keep a calm tone and avoid defensive attitudes such as crossing your arms or rolling your eyes, as this can exacerbate tension.

<u>Give space for both to speak:</u> It's crucial that both parties feel they have the time and space to express their thoughts. Interrupting the other or ignoring their point of view will only increase frustration and make it harder to resolve the conflict.

3. Negotiation: Finding mutually beneficial solutions

Negotiating is not about winning or losing. In a relationship, the goal is to find a solution where both people feel that their needs have been heard and valued. To achieve this, it is essential to be willing to compromise, without feeling that one of you is sacrificing too much.

Strategies for effective negotiation:

<u>Focus on the problem, not the person:</u> When arguing, focus on the specific problem that is affecting you, rather than attacking the other's character. This makes it easier to focus on solutions rather than blame. If one of you is irritated by a bad day, it is preferable to say, "I'm worried about your stress, it could hurt you," rather than accuse him or her of having a "dog-like temper."

<u>Identify underlying interests:</u> Disagreements often arise because people do not communicate what is bothering them. For example, an argument about expenses could be related to deeper concerns about financial security. Identifying real interests helps find solutions that address the underlying needs of both.

<u>Look for win-win solutions:</u> Compromise doesn't mean one person has to give in on everything. Both can work

together to find a solution that both feel satisfied with. This may require creativity and patience, but it's crucial to maintaining equity in the relationship.

4. Empathy in times of tension: Putting yourself in another's shoes

Empathy is the ability to put yourself in another's shoes and understand how they feel. During a conflict, empathy can be difficult to apply, especially when both are feeling hurt or frustrated. However, it is a powerful tool to defuse tension and promote more constructive dialogue.

How to practice empathy during conflict:

<u>Listen before you respond:</u> Instead of preparing to refute your partner's point of view, try to listen to what they are saying and what they are feeling. Ask yourself, "Why is he or she so upset? What is he or she worried about?"

<u>Validate the other's feelings:</u> Validation doesn't mean agreeing, but rather acknowledging that the other person has a right to feel that way. Phrases like "I can see that you are frustrated by this" or "I understand that you feel that way" can help ease tension and open space for a more respectful dialogue.

<u>Acknowledge one's role in the conflict:</u> Accepting responsibility for our actions and attitudes can quickly defuse an argument. Admit if you have made a mistake and offer a sincere apology. This shows maturity and a genuine willingness to improve the situation.

5. Time out Take a breather when conflict escalates
Sometimes when an argument escalates too much, it
is helpful to take a "breather" to calm down before
continuing. This doesn't mean avoiding the issue, but
rather taking a moment to process emotions and
approach the conflict with a clearer mind.

How to apply a healthy "time out":

Announce it assertively: Saying something like, "I need
a moment to calm down, but I'll be back in 10 minutes
so we can continue talking" is a way to communicate
the need for space without abandoning the discussion.

Use the time to reflect, not build up resentment:
During the time out, focus on calming down and
reflecting on the conflict. Avoid feeding negative
thoughts or looking for ways to "win" the argument.

Return to the topic when both are calm: After some
time to breathe, return to the conversation with a
calmer, more rational approach. This increases the
chances of finding a solution rather than escalating the
conflict.

**6. Resolve disagreements without resentment: The
power of forgiveness**
Resentment can build up when conflicts are not
handled properly or when arguments turn into power
battles. Learning to resolve disagreements in a way
that both parties can put the conflict behind them is
essential to maintaining a healthy relationship.

Strategies to avoid resentment:

Don't drag past conflicts around: If an issue has been resolved, don't bring it up in future discussions. Letting go of past conflicts is key to avoiding built-up resentments.

Practice mutual forgiveness: Forgiveness is essential to healing a relationship after a conflict. This doesn't mean forgetting what happened, but rather letting go of resentment and committing to moving forward together.

The Role of Mental Health

Mental health plays a crucial role in developing and maintaining healthy personal and romantic relationships. Research indicates that people who have positive relationships tend to experience greater happiness and productivity, as well as better health outcomes.

Poor mental health can lead to chronic emotional stress, which has been associated with a variety of health problems, including heart disease and increased risk of mortality.

A lack of social connections can increase the risk of depression and cognitive decline, highlighting the importance of social support networks for mental health.

The benefits of social support are therefore reciprocal, with both those who give and those who receive it experiencing life-enhancing effects from their interactions.

Consequently, fostering enriching relationships protects mental well-being and overall health, highlighting the interconnection between emotional support and physical well-being.

Individual Growth and Self-Care

Taking care of mental health through self-care practices is critical to maintaining a healthy relationship. Encouraging individual growth, such as exercising regularly and fostering emotional balance, allows partners to better support each other and improves the overall health of the relationship.

When people prioritize their well-being, they can positively contribute to their relationships, creating a nurturing and balanced dynamic that fosters resilience and understanding.

Seeking professional help

In situations where conflict arises or relationships become complicated, it may be beneficial to seek professional help through couples therapy or individual therapy. A mental health professional can provide couples with essential tools to effectively address conflict and improve communication skills.

If one partner is resistant to therapy, the other may find it helpful to conduct individual sessions to focus on their own needs and well-being. Cognitive behavioral therapy (CBT) is an effective modality that helps people understand the roots of their conflicts and manage negative feelings that can arise during difficult times.

Conflict as an opportunity for growth

Differences and conflict are not signs of failure in a relationship; They are opportunities to learn more about oneself and each other. Properly handling these disagreements, through respectful communication, empathy, and negotiation, defines the quality of a relationship. When couples confront their differences constructively, they not only resolve problems but also strengthen their connection and grow together.

Chapter 5
Building
Emotional Intimacy

In any meaningful relationship, whether romantic, familial, or friendly, emotional connection is the core that sustains the bond between two people. Beyond physical attraction or shared interests, what truly deepens a relationship is the ability to connect emotionally. This connection is based on vulnerability, mutual support, and understanding of each other's emotions.

In this chapter, we will explore how to foster emotional intimacy and how these key aspects help strengthen a deep and meaningful relationship.

Psychological Theories Relevant to Healthy Relationships

Emotional bonds between people are fundamental in the development of intimate relationships, whether romantic, familial, or friendly. These connections are influenced by various psychological dynamics that determine how we relate, seek affection, and deal with emotional closeness. Among the most important theories are:

1. Attachment theory
Developed by psychiatrist and psychoanalyst John Bowlby, attachment theory focuses on how early experiences with caregivers (such as parents) affect

how people relate emotionally to others throughout their lives. According to this theory, the attachment style we develop in childhood influences how we bond in our adult relationships.

Types of attachment:

Secure attachment: People with a secure attachment are usually comfortable with intimacy and independence. In childhood, these individuals experienced a reliable and consistent bond with their caregivers. In adult life, they trust their partners, feel secure in their relationships, and handle emotional conflicts better.

Anxious attachment: People with anxious attachment tend to worry a lot about being abandoned or rejected. They often need constant reassurance and attention in their relationships. This type of attachment arises from inconsistent parenting, where care and affection are not always secure or predictable.

Avoidant attachment: People with avoidant attachment tend to maintain an emotional distance in relationships, preferring independence and avoiding intimacy. These people may have grown up in environments where affection and emotional support were limited.

Disorganized attachment: This type of attachment is a mix of anxious and avoidant behaviors, often stemming from traumatic or chaotic experiences in childhood. People with disorganized attachments may feel an internal conflict between wanting closeness and at the same time fearing it.

2. Codependency

Codependency is a form of relationship in which one person feels emotionally dependent on the well-being or behavior of another. This dynamic is common in relationships where one partner has addiction, abuse, or mental health issues, and the other person takes on the role of "caretaker" or "rescuer." However, codependency can also appear in relationships where these problems do not exist and is usually characterized by an extreme desire to please or control the relationship.

Characteristics of codependency:

<u>Lack of emotional boundaries:</u> Codependent people often have difficulty setting clear boundaries, which leads them to constantly put the needs of others before their own.

<u>Need for approval:</u> Codependent people often seek constant validation and recognition from others, basing their self-esteem on external approval.

<u>Control and dependence</u>: Although the term suggests dependence, many codependent people try to control the emotions or actions of others to feel safe, which can create toxic dynamics in the relationship.

3. Love and emotional dependence

Emotional dependence is a state in which one person depends on another to meet all their emotional and affection needs. It is often confused with love, but rather than being a connection based on reciprocity and mutual growth, emotional dependency is based on the constant need for the other person to feel complete or secure.

Signs of emotional dependency:

<u>Fear of abandonment:</u> A person with emotional dependency may experience intense anxiety at the thought of their partner or friend moving away, leading to possessive behaviors or excessive jealousy.

<u>Difficulty being alone:</u> Emotionally dependent individuals often feel incomplete or empty when they are not with the person they are dependent on.

<u>Idealization of partner:</u> They may see their partner as the only source of happiness, ignoring their desires, goals, and individual well-being.

4. Interdependence: The healthy balance

In contrast to emotional dependence and codependency, interdependence is a more balanced and healthier model of emotional bonding. In an interdependent relationship, both individuals maintain their identity and autonomy but are deeply connected and committed to each other. This type of relationship is characterized by mutual support without the loss of personal independence.

Keys to interdependence:

<u>Respect for autonomy:</u> Interdependent people support each other, but they also respect individual boundaries

and allow their partners or friends to grow independently.

<u>Open communication:</u> In interdependent relationships, communication is clear and direct, which prevents misunderstandings and fosters a relationship based on trust.

<u>Mutual Support:</u> Rather than seeking to control or change the other, interdependent people support each other in their personal goals and desires, creating an environment of mutual growth.

Adult Attachment Bonds and Friendship

Relationships between friends are also influenced by attachment styles, although in a less intense context than in romantic relationships. Friendship can be a safe space for people to practice and develop emotional skills. A secure attachment style, for example, facilitates friendships where there is trust and mutual support, while an avoidant style can lead to superficial or distant friendships.

Understanding the different types of emotional attachment is crucial to cultivating healthy and balanced relationships. Attachment theory teaches us that our early experiences influence how we connect with others, but also that it is possible to change and heal attachment patterns. Recognizing codependency or emotional dependence is the first step in transforming these dynamics into healthier relationships based on interdependence. The key to any successful emotional bond is balance: maintaining our independence while building a deep bond of mutual support and understanding.

Ultimately, the emotional bonds we form can be a source of personal growth and happiness if handled with awareness, respect, and love. Understanding these attachment styles can help couples navigate relationship dynamics more effectively, fostering a deeper understanding of each other's needs and enhancing emotional connections.

Characteristics of Healthy Emotional Connection

1. Emotional Connection as the Foundation of a Strong Relationship

Emotional connection is the invisible bond that allows us to feel close to another person. It gives us the feeling of being seen, heard, and understood on a deep level. In romantic relationships, this type of intimacy not only strengthens love but also creates a sense of security and trust that can endure over time.

When people feel emotionally connected, they can share their deepest thoughts and feelings without fear of judgment or rejection. This opening creates a space for mutual growth and reinforces the ability of the couple or friends to overcome difficulties together.

Remember: You can ask another person for many things; but never for them to love you, because that does not depend on the other person's will, but on whether that feeling exists in them towards you. Therefore, becoming bitter about a rejection, or trying to get the other person to come back to us, is often a pointless battle. Think about it, the same thing happens the other way around because we will always see ourselves with the right to follow our path, no matter how much the other person suffers.

2. Vulnerability: The First Step to Emotional Intimacy

Being vulnerable is essential to establishing a deep emotional connection. However, in many relationships, vulnerability can be seen as a weakness, when in fact it is an act of great courage. Being vulnerable means exposing yourself emotionally, and sharing your innermost fears, insecurities, and desires. Although this may seem risky, it is the only way to build true emotional closeness.

Don't confuse vulnerability with a lack of masculinity or feminine manipulation; it is about both of you showing yourselves as complete people: what you like and what you don't, what you think, feel, and fear.

Why vulnerability strengthens emotional connection:

It builds trust: When a person opens and shares something vulnerable, they are saying to the other, "I trust you enough to show you this part of me." This, in turn, fosters a response of trust and reciprocity.

It fosters empathy: By sharing our vulnerabilities, we allow the other to understand our emotions, generating empathy and understanding.

Break emotional barriers: Many times, we avoid being vulnerable for fear of being hurt. However, emotional intimacy can only develop if we break those barriers and allow the other to see us in our entirety, with both our strengths and weaknesses.

Tips to foster vulnerability in the relationship:

Share your emotions, not just facts: It's not just about telling what has happened to you, but how it has made you feel. "I feel insecure when we don't talk for a long time," is deeper than "We haven't talked much lately."

Be honest about your fears: Sharing your fears and insecurities doesn't make you weak, it makes you human. Expressing these feelings helps create an atmosphere of acceptance and support.

Listen without judgment: If your partner or friend decides to open emotionally, it's crucial to respond without judgment. Empathy and validation are key to making vulnerability constructive in a relationship.

3. Mutual support as a pillar of emotional connection

Mutual support is a tangible manifestation of emotional connection in a deep relationship. This support involves not only being there in times of crisis but also in small daily difficulties, triumphs, and emotional challenges. Knowing that we can count on the other person, and vice versa is what makes a relationship a source of security and emotional strength.

Mutual support in practice:

<u>Active listening:</u> One of the most powerful ways to emotionally support someone is to simply listen to them. Sometimes, all we need is for someone to listen to us and validate our feelings, without needing to look for immediate solutions.

<u>Being present in difficult times:</u> Emotional support is not just about words, but about actions. Being physically there for the other in times of difficulty, such as a personal or work crisis, demonstrates a genuine commitment to the other's well-being.

<u>Celebrating each other's successes:</u> Support should not only appear in times of pain or frustration. Celebrating successes, achievements, and moments of joy strengthens the emotional connection, creating a positive environment in the relationship.

4. Understanding the Other's Emotions: Empathy and Emotional Communication

Emotional understanding in a relationship goes beyond listening; it is about putting yourself in the other person's shoes, feeling what they feel, and acting accordingly. Empathy, the ability to understand and share the other person's feelings, is one of the most important components of an emotionally connected relationship.

How to develop emotional empathy:

<u>Listen without interrupting:</u> Let the other person fully express what they are feeling before offering your

perspective. This will make them feel like their emotions are important.

<u>Validate their feelings:</u> Sometimes, we just need to hear, "I understand why you feel that way." Validation doesn't mean agreeing, but simply acknowledging that the other person's emotion is valid.

<u>Ask questions to better understand:</u> If you don't fully understand how the other person feels, instead of assuming, ask questions with the goal of better understanding. "Why did this make you feel that way?" or "What worries you most about this situation?" are examples of questions that can open the door to greater emotional understanding.

5. The power of shared time: Creating moments of emotional connection

Emotional connection doesn't always happen amid big confessions or moments of crisis. Often, it is cultivated in the small, everyday moments: a conversation before bed, a dinner at home, or just being together without distractions. Sharing quality time allows you to strengthen the emotional bond and maintain the connection.

Ways to foster daily emotional connection:

<u>Daily rituals:</u> Establishing small daily rituals, such as talking about how the day went, watching a series together, or going for a walk, reinforces the sense of connection and belonging.

Physical touch: In a romantic relationship, physical contact, such as hugs or caresses, can be a powerful way to reinforce the emotional bond. In other relationships, such as friendship or family, a gesture of affection or a simple pat on the back can convey support and connection.

Being present: In a world full of distractions, simply being present and giving full attention to the other person is a powerful way to strengthen emotional connection.

Emotional connection as a source of strength

Emotional connection is the core that fuels the deepest and most meaningful relationships. Through vulnerability, mutual support, and empathy, we create a safe space where we can be authentic, share our most intimate emotions, and grow together with the other person. Fostering this connection not only strengthens the bond between two people but also enriches their emotional lives, creating a relationship that can meet any challenge with resilience and understanding.

Ultimately, truly deep relationships are not based solely on what we do or say, but on how we connect emotionally, how we care for each other's emotional well-being, and how we build together a space where both can be themselves.

Chapter 6
Growing Together: Fostering Individual and Couple Development

A healthy relationship is not only about the connection between two people but also about how that relationship fosters each person's well-being and personal growth.

In a balanced couple, both partners can thrive, develop, and reach their full individual potential while growing together as a team. However, finding a balance between personal growth and joint growth is key to maintaining a harmonious and fulfilling relationship. In this chapter, we explore how to achieve this balance and how a healthy relationship strengthens both the couple and the individuals within it.

Strategies to foster healthy relationships

To cultivate and maintain healthy relationships, people can adopt several strategies:

<u>Engage in shared activities:</u> Trying new hobbies or interests together can foster connection and create shared memories. Learning a language, dancing, going to the gym, going for a walk, going to the movies, etc., are highly rewarding activities that can be done in company.

<u>Prioritize quality time:</u> Spending dedicated time together without distractions can strengthen emotional bonds and reinforce the relationship.

<u>Seek professional guidance if necessary:</u> If challenges arise, consulting a therapist can provide insight into how to address difficulties and determine when it may be necessary to seek further support or reevaluate the relationship dynamics.

By focusing on these elements, individuals can cultivate healthier relationships that provide emotional support, mutual respect, and lasting satisfaction.

Confronting Misconceptions

1. The "We" Over "I" Myth

One of the common mistakes in relationships is thinking that for a couple to thrive, both partners must sacrifice parts of themselves in favor of "we." Although compromise is essential, a healthy relationship does not require individuals to give up their identity, passions, or goals. The strongest relationships are those in which both individuals can grow and develop personally, which positively contributes to joint growth.

Myth: "If I focus on myself, I will be neglecting the relationship."
Fact: When you care about your personal development, you bring a more complete, happy, and fulfilled version of yourself to the relationship, which in turn enriches your connection with your partner.

2. Personal growth as a foundation for a stronger relationship

Personal growth involves working on yourself, your goals, your physical and emotional well-being, and your sense of identity. To have a healthy relationship, it is essential for each partner to feel individually fulfilled. Doing so prevents emotional dependency, allowing for a relationship based on mutual respect and support, rather than neediness or insecurity. The goal is to find the best version of yourself and offer it to your partner.

Keys to fostering personal growth within the relationship:

Time for yourself: Having time for yourself, whether for hobbies, exercise, or reflection, is vital for your mental and emotional health. The couple does not have to share every moment; giving space to individuality strengthens autonomy. This item includes meeting with friends, which do not necessarily have to be the same as those shared with the couple.

Setting individual goals: Each member of the couple should have personal goals and dreams, whether in the professional, creative, or personal well-being sphere. These personal goals not only give meaning to your life outside the relationship but also provide personal satisfaction and a sense of purpose.

Developing self-esteem: Working on your self-esteem, without depending exclusively on the validation of the partner, is essential for a healthy relationship. People with strong self-esteem can provide more support and understanding to their partner since they do not depend on the relationship to define their self-worth.

3. Growing Together: Building a Shared Life Project
Growing together involves the evolution of the relationship as a team. Like personal growth, growing together requires effort, dedication, and a shared vision. In a strong relationship, both partners work together to achieve common goals, support each other, and build a life that reflects their collective values and desires.

Key aspects of growing together:

Setting deep shared goals: In addition to individual goals, couples should also have common goals, such as building a home, traveling, starting a family, or achieving financial stability. These goals give a sense of purpose to the relationship and help both partners feel aligned in their vision of the future.

Making decisions together: Joint decision-making is essential for growing as a couple. This does not mean that every decision must be made by consensus, but important decisions, such as moving, investments, or family plans, should be discussed and agreed upon by both parties.

Overcoming challenges as a team: Challenges in a relationship, whether emotional, financial, or external, offer opportunities for joint growth. Rather than seeing obstacles as threats, healthy couples face them together, strengthening their resilience and commitment to each other.

4. The balance between autonomy and interdependence

The balance between personal growth and joint growth is achieved through a healthy interdependent relationship. In this dynamic, both partners can maintain their autonomy while supporting each other to thrive. It is not about emotional dependence, where one is completely dependent on the other for their well-being, nor about total independence, where both function as if they were alone. The key is interdependence: a relationship where both individuals are independent but choose to support each other.

How to foster interdependence in a relationship:

<u>Support without suffocation:</u> It is important to support your partner in their goals and projects without intervening excessively or imposing your expectations. Offer support, advice, and love, but respect their decisions and processes.

<u>Encourage individuality:</u> Valuing and encouraging your partner's interests, hobbies, and personal goals is a sign of respect and love. This allows your partner to feel free to develop without feeling like they are neglecting the relationship.

<u>Sharing without losing themselves:</u> Finding ways to share life without losing your identity is essential. Enjoying time together and building a shared future does not mean losing sight of who you are as an individual.

5. The impact of personal growth on the relationship

When both partners strive to grow individually, this brings multiple benefits to the relationship. By feeling fulfilled and secure in their identity, they can approach the relationship with a more open mind, higher self-esteem, and an ability to face challenges with more resilience.

Benefits of personal growth in the relationship:

<u>Greater relationship satisfaction:</u> People who feel good about themselves and their individual lives tend to feel more satisfied in their relationships. They do not need to rely on their partner for their happiness, which takes the pressure off the relationship and allows for a more natural and fluid connection.

<u>Reduced codependency:</u> Personal growth reduces the tendency toward codependency, where one person is emotionally dependent on the other to feel complete. In a healthy relationship, both partners can support each other without needing to "complete" each other.

<u>More balanced relationship:</u> When both partners have a rich life outside of the relationship, imbalances where one person gives more of themselves than the other are avoided. This fosters a greater sense of fairness and respect in the relationship.

6. Supporting each other in personal growth

A healthy relationship not only allows for individual growth but also encourages it. When both partners support each other in their goals and dreams, the relationship becomes a source of motivation and strength for both.

Ways to support your partner's personal growth:

<u>Encourage and celebrate their achievements</u>: Actively supporting your partner in their projects and goals and celebrating their successes, big or small, is a powerful way to show your commitment to their well-being.

<u>Listen and be present</u>: When your partner faces challenges in their personal growth, listen and offer emotional support. Being present during difficult times strengthens the bond between you both.

<u>Avoid competition:</u> Sometimes, one partner's personal growth can create insecurities in the other. It's important to avoid falling into a competitive dynamic. Instead, celebrate your partner's success as if it were your achievement, remembering that you are both growing together in different areas.

Growing Together and Separately

A healthy relationship does not require sacrificing the "I" for the "we." Instead, both individuals should be able to grow separately and together, supporting each other in their personal development and shared goals. By fostering this balance, the relationship is not only strengthened, but it also enriches the lives of both, creating a space in which both can thrive, achieve their goals, and enjoy a deep and meaningful connection.

When each partner feels fulfilled and valued, the relationship becomes a source of strength, growth, and unconditional love. The key is to maintain the balance between personal growth and joint growth, allowing both to flourish, both individually and as a couple.

Chapter 7
Breaking Toxic Patterns
and Healing the Relationship

Every relationship faces challenges, but some behavioral patterns can be especially damaging if not identified and addressed early. These patterns, such as resentment, codependency, and other negative dynamics, can erode trust and connection between people, affecting the health of the relationship. Recognizing and working to break these cycles is key to regaining harmony and well-being for both individuals within the couple. In this final chapter, we will discuss these patterns, how to identify them, and offer tools to overcome them and heal the relationship.

1. Identifying harmful patterns in a relationship

Harmful patterns are not always immediately obvious. Often, they develop gradually and become normalized over time. They may emerge as defense mechanisms or strategies to deal with problems, but rather than resolving them, they tend to perpetuate them. It is essential to learn to identify them and recognize when these behaviors are negatively affecting the relationship.

Signs of damaging patterns:

Negative communication: Sarcasm, constant criticism, passive-aggressive comments, or verbal aggression are signs of a destructive dynamic.

Accumulated resentment: Resentment grows when needs are not expressed or feel ignored, and it becomes an emotional barrier that prevents closeness.

Submission-manipulation: As we have pointed out, this situation manifests when one person depends excessively on the other for their emotional well-being, leading to dynamics of control and personal sacrifice.

Repetitive conflict cycles: The same arguments or disagreements that are not resolved and re-emerge, often worsening over time.

Emotional withdrawal or avoidance: Prolonged silence or unwillingness to face problems can be an indication that there are patterns of avoidance that damage the relationship.

Irreconcilable personalities or behavior: It often happens that after the stage of falling in love, the true characteristics of people come to light, whether in their character, mannerisms, or behaviors, which are unbearable to the other, and which the executor is not willing to modify or put up for debate.

2. Resentment: A silent threat

Resentment is one of the most common and damaging patterns in a relationship. It usually accumulates when one or both people feel that their needs are not being met or that they have sacrificed too much without receiving adequate recognition or support. The problem with resentment is that it grows silently, gradually affecting the way one person perceives the other, eroding love and mutual respect.

How to identify resentment:

• Unexpressed feelings of frustration or anger that build up over time.
• Tendency to avoid important topics to avoid generating conflict, which leads to an accumulation of unresolved tensions.
• Disregard or indifference to the other person's needs and feelings.
• Recurrence of thoughts like "I always do everything" or "I'm never valued."

Tools to overcome resentment:

<u>Open communication:</u> Expressing your feelings honestly and without attacking the other person is essential to release resentment. You can use phrases like "I feel frustrated because I need more support in the X area."

<u>Mutual forgiveness:</u> Forgiveness does not mean forgetting, but releasing the emotional weight that resentment brings with it. Practicing forgiveness will allow you to let go of accumulated anger and be more willing to rebuild the relationship.

<u>Set clear barriers:</u> If resentment arises from a lack of equity in responsibilities, it is crucial to establish clear boundaries and roles in the relationship to prevent one member from carrying more than they can handle.

3. When the relationship becomes a source of imbalance

Lack of self-esteem and submission is a dynamic in which one person depends emotionally on the other to the point of losing their identity. While healthy interdependence is necessary for a strong relationship, codependency leads to a loss of autonomy and often to controlling or manipulative dynamics.

Signs of codependency:

• Constantly needing approval from one's partner to feel valid or accepted.
• Constantly sacrificing one's desires, needs, or well-being for the other, without reciprocation.
• Feeling a compulsive need to "fix" or rescue the other, even at the cost of one's well-being.
• Fear of being alone or without the relationship, which creates excessive emotional dependence.

Strategies to break codependency:

<u>Developing personal autonomy:</u> Each person needs to work on their emotional independence and developing a rich life outside the relationship. This may include hobbies, personal goals, or social activities.

<u>Individual or couples therapy:</u> Therapy can help dismantle codependency patterns and learn new ways to relate in a more balanced and healthy way.

<u>Encouraging self-exploration:</u> Asking yourself what you need and want as an individual will help you develop greater self-awareness and set healthy boundaries in the relationship.

<u>Strengthen Self-Affirmation:</u> Instead of constantly seeking external validation, practicing self-affirmation will allow you to feel secure and validated without relying on your partner's approval.

4. Conflict Cycles: How to Handle Them Effectively

Conflicts in a relationship are inevitable, but what matters is how they are handled. A destructive conflict pattern can repeat itself when problems are not properly resolved, leading to cyclical arguments that drain the couple's emotional energy.

How to Identify a Destructive Conflict Cycle:

• The same arguments arise repeatedly, without reaching solutions.
• During conflicts, personal attacks are resorted to instead of addressing the real problem.
• One or both partners emotionally withdraw or avoid the conflict, making the situation worse.
• The "silent treatment" or avoidance is used as a way to control or punish.

Tools for managing conflict:

<u>Active listening:</u> Listening to the other person without interrupting and trying to understand their perspective is key to preventing conflicts from escalating.

<u>Non-violent communication:</u> Speaking from the "I" instead of the "you" is essential to avoid the blame game. Phrases like "I feel sad when this happens" are more effective than "You always do this wrong."

<u>Time-outs during conflict:</u> If the discussion becomes too intense, taking time to cool down before continuing to talk can prevent the conflict from escalating.

Seeking solutions instead of winning: The goal of an argument should not be to "win," but to find a solution that works for both of you. This requires empathy, compromise, and a willingness to compromise when necessary.

5. Healing the relationship: Tools for Recovery

Once harmful patterns have been identified and worked through, it is important to adopt practices that help heal the relationship and prevent those patterns from resurfacing. This requires a conscious effort from both parties to nurture the relationship and promote a mutually supportive environment.

Herramientas para sanar:

<u>Couples therapy</u>: If patterns are deep or difficult to change, couples therapy can offer a safe space for both of you to express your concerns and learn new ways to interact.

<u>Practicing gratitude:</u> Fostering a positive environment in the relationship through mutual gratitude helps reduce feelings of resentment and frustration. Taking the time to acknowledge your partner's small gestures and efforts can have a big impact on the dynamic.

<u>Reviewing relationship agreements:</u> Over time, needs and expectations change. It's helpful to regularly sit down and review relationship agreements and

commitments to make sure you're both aligned and happy with the course of the relationship.

<u>Commitment to change:</u> Transforming harmful patterns isn't something that happens overnight. It requires a consistent commitment from both parties to changing attitudes and behaviors, and a willingness to work at it on an ongoing basis.

Healing to Grow

Harmful patterns in a relationship can seem overwhelming, but with the right effort, it is possible to break these cycles and heal. The key is awareness, a willingness to change, and a mutual commitment to grow both individually and as a couple. Through open communication, respect for personal boundaries, and mutual support, couples can overcome destructive dynamics and build a healthier, more balanced, and fulfilling relationship.

The process of healing a relationship not only strengthens the bond between the two but also allows each individual to grow and develop in an environment of love and respect.

As a summary of this book, these are the tips for building a healthy relationship:

Mutual respect: Value each other's opinions, feelings, and boundaries.

Trust: Believe in the other person's integrity and good intentions.

Honesty: Be sincere in words and actions.

Open communication: Express feelings and needs clearly and assertively.

Mutual support: Be there for each other in good and bad times.

Equality: Both members have a say in decision-making.

Communication is the bridge that connects people. Through it, we express our feelings, resolve conflicts, and build intimacy. Effective communication involves:

Active listening: Paying full attention to what the other person says, without interrupting or judging.

Empathy: Putting yourself in the other person's shoes and trying to understand their feelings.

Assertiveness: Expressing your needs and opinions clearly and respectfully, without blaming or attacking.

Conflict resolution: Facing problems constructively, seeking mutually beneficial solutions.

Tips to improve communication and strengthen relationships:

Choose the right time: Avoid talking about important topics when you are tired, stressed, or distracted.

Create a safe environment: Find a quiet, private place where you can both express yourself without feeling judged.

Use "I" instead of "you": When expressing your feelings, use first-person statements to avoid blaming the other person. For example, instead of saying, "You always keep me waiting," say, "I get frustrated when I have to wait a long time."

Validate the other person's feelings: Acknowledge and validate the other person's emotions, even if you don't agree with them.

Practice active listening: Maintain eye contact, nod, and paraphrase what the other person has said to make sure you have understood correctly.

Avoid generalizations: Instead of saying, "You always do the same thing," use concrete examples to illustrate your point.

Take breaks: If a conversation is getting too intense, take a short break to calm down and come back to it later.

Seek professional help if necessary: A therapist can provide tools and strategies to improve communication and resolve conflicts.

In addition to good communication, there are other ways to strengthen relationships:

Spend quality time together: Do activities that you both enjoy.

Show appreciation: Express your gratitude and admiration for each other.

Celebrate accomplishments: Recognize and celebrate the successes of your partner or friends.

Forgive: Letting go of resentment is essential to moving forward in a relationship.

Take care of yourself: A happy and healthy person can build stronger relationships.

<u>Remember:</u> Building healthy relationships requires effort and commitment from both parties. By improving communication and practicing the skills mentioned above, you will be able to strengthen your bonds and enjoy more satisfying relationships.

But we know that in this same universe, there are lights and shadows, and no matter how much you put into practice everything pointed out in this book, humans behave erratically and subjectively, so, just as you aspire to a strong and lasting relationship, you also have to be prepared for when it doesn't work, and the insistence becomes toxic... or even worse, with more tragic endings.

Indicators that a romantic relationship has come to an end: How to recognize it and face the separation peacefully

Romantic relationships go through different stages, from the initial euphoria to the challenges that arise over time. However, not all relationships are meant to last, and it is essential to recognize the indicators that a relationship has come to an end. Insisting on maintaining a relationship that is no longer healthy can cause emotional damage to both parties. You should be aware of the signs that a relationship might be ending, be aware of the dangers of holding on to an unsustainable relationship, and how to carry out a peaceful separation while healthily coping with grief.

Indicators that a relationship has reached its breaking point

Although every relationship is unique, some common signs suggest a relationship has reached its breaking point:

Lack of effective communication: Communication is one of the fundamental pillars of any relationship. If conversations have become monotonous, filled with unresolved or non-existent conflict, and neither party is willing to work to improve it, it is a sign that the relationship might be exhausted.

Emotional disconnection: The absence of emotional intimacy, affection, or caring, and the feeling of being emotionally distant, are clear indicators that a couple has lost the bond that united them. When the interest in sharing time or supporting each other disappears, the relationship is in danger.

<u>Resentment and constant blame</u>: Accumulated resentment is one of the greatest enemies of a relationship. If every interaction is tinged with blame, criticism, and hostility, the emotional wounds are likely to be too deep to be repaired. The relationship becomes a cycle of pain rather than a space of support.

<u>Lack of trust and loyalty</u>: Trust is essential in a loving relationship. If trust has been broken and there is no will to rebuild it, or if the relationship is marked by deception, constant jealousy, or disloyalty, the relationship may be over.

<u>Absence of joint growth</u>: If one or both people feel that the relationship is preventing them from growing as individuals or achieving their personal goals, this may be a sign that the relationship is no longer beneficial. When dreams and aspirations do not align or are hindered, the relationship may be stifling personal development.

<u>Irreconcilable differences</u>: Sometimes fundamental differences in values, beliefs, or long-term desires (for example, whether you want children) can make it impossible for a relationship to continue, even if there is love.

The Danger of Dwelling on a Relationship That's Over

Holding on to a relationship that has lost its essence can be emotionally and psychologically damaging to both parties. Some of the dangers include:

Deteriorated Self-Esteem: Staying in a dysfunctional relationship can severely affect self-esteem as people may feel unappreciated or trapped. Emotional burnout and lack of validation can lead to a sense of inadequacy.

Emotional Burnout: Conflictual relationships are emotionally draining. Dwelling on an unsalvageable relationship can prolong suffering, create more conflict, and increase pain rather than resolve it.

Denial of Opportunities: By staying in a relationship that is no longer working, people close the door to new opportunities for themselves, whether emotionally, personally, or even in other, healthier relationships.

How to Carry Out a Peaceful Breakup

A breakup doesn't have to be a process filled with pain and conflict. With the right approach, it is possible to carry out a breakup respectfully and peacefully. Here are some key steps:

Honest and clear communication: Talking openly about feelings and reasons for the separation is crucial. Both parties should have the opportunity to express their emotions without resorting to accusations or blame. Clarity and respect in the conversation can avoid misunderstandings and facilitate a peaceful breakup.

Accepting reality: Both parties must accept that the relationship has come to an end and that continuing will only prolong the pain. It is important to recognize that ending the relationship is not a failure, but a step toward healing and personal growth.

Staying calm and avoiding conflict: It is normal to feel a great emotional burden during a separation, but it is crucial to avoid heated arguments. If a conversation becomes too tense, it is best to take a break and return when both are calmer.

Seeking help if necessary: If the separation process becomes complicated, it is useful to seek the mediation of a therapist or counselor to facilitate the transition healthily and minimize emotional pain.

Taking care of the practicalities: In addition to the emotional, separations entail practical changes. Whether it's dividing property, and responsibilities, or making decisions about children together, addressing these issues rationally and without resentment can prevent prolonged conflict.

Coping with grief after a separation

After a separation, it's normal to feel sadness, confusion, and loss. Grief is a natural process, and coping with it healthily is key to emotional recovery.

Allowing yourself to feel the pain: Grief is inevitable after the end of a relationship. It's important to allow yourself to feel sadness and pain without repressing your emotions. Crying, reflecting, and talking to people close to you can help you process the loss.

Time to heal: Taking time to be alone and heal before starting a new relationship is crucial. This allows you to reflect on the past relationship, learn from the experience, and heal emotionally before opening up to new possibilities.

Seeking support: Talking to friends, family, or a therapist can be a great help during the grieving process. Sharing feelings with others can ease the pain and offer new perspectives.

Focus on personal growth: After a breakup, it can be helpful to focus on self-care and personal growth. This may include exploring new activities, learning new skills, or rediscovering forgotten hobbies.

Recognizing that a relationship has come to an end is an act of courage and self-awareness. Insisting on maintaining a dysfunctional relationship can be damaging to both parties, while a peaceful separation offers the opportunity to heal and grow. Through honest communication, mutual respect, and emotional support, it is possible to face the end of a relationship in a healthy way, allowing both people to find peace and move on with their lives.

However, many times an early separation based on pride or weakness in overcoming adversity can result in regret and self-criticism later, from which there is no return.

Always remember "Communication is the fundamental pillar of all our relationships." Most human problems originate in communication, or the lack of it. So, if you are tired of misunderstandings, conflicts, and unsatisfactory relationships, come back to this book as many times as you need, as it will provide you with the tools and knowledge necessary to improve your communication skills and strengthen your emotional bonds.

Be happy! Enjoy life